MW00411975

FRUIT JARS & Fireflies

DOWN-HOME DEVOTIONS
TO LIGHT YOUR PATH

KEN PETERSEN
General Editor

Tyndale House Publishers
Carol Stream, Illinois

LIVING EXPRESSIONS COLLECTION

Living Expressions invites you to explore God's Word and express your creativity in ways that are refreshing to the spirit and restorative to the soul.

Visit Tyndale online at tyndale.com.

TYNDALE, Tyndale's quill logo, *Living Expressions*, and the Living Expressions logo are registered trademarks of Tyndale House Ministries.

Fruit Jars and Fireflies: Down-Home Devotions to Light Your Path

Designed by Ron C. Kaufmann

For information about special discounts for bulk purchases, please contact Tyndale House Publishers at csresponse@tyndale.com, or call 1-800-323-9400.

ISBN 978-1-4964-4449-3

Printed in China

26	25	24	23	22	21	20
7	6	5	4	3	2	1

Contents

The people who sat in darkness

have seen a great light.

And for those who lived in the land

where death casts its shadow,

a light has shined.

MATTHEW 4:16

Shine your light on those around you

Remember how much fun you had as a kid on hot summer nights, capturing fireflies (some call them lightning bugs) and putting them in fruit jars? The different mix of chemicals inside each type of firefly produces unique patterns of light. Did you know that you, too, emit a one-of-a-kind pattern of light to the world if God's Spirit is abiding within you? In the darkness of this world, you have a special, God-given sparkle that can pierce the night. But the Bible warns against hiding your light "under a basket" (Matthew 5:15). So many things are fixin' to dull your sparkle—people who shame your faith, the distractions of daily life, the temptations of the world. So be careful not to lose your glow. Instead, focus on Jesus each day and let him shine through your unique personality. Then watch him brighten the lives of those around you.

Let your light shine before others, so that they may see your good works and give glory to your Father who is in heaven.

MATTHEW 5:16, ESV

When trouble surrounds you

The play and film *The Music Man* features a song titled "Pick-a-Little, Talk-a-Little," which depicts ladies from the town gossiping like chickens—pick, pick, pick; talk, talk, talk. Are you feeling overwhelmed by those pecking at you with a hundred little stings and barbs? Well, don't count your chickens before you're pecked. Proverbs 29:25 says, "Fearing people is a dangerous trap, but trusting the LORD means safety." Seek to silence all those "pick-a-little" troubles by spending time with the Lord in his Word and in prayer. Let him reassure you of his care for you, and ask him for the strength to "love your enemies and pray for those who persecute you" (Matthew 5:44, NIV).

LORD, don't hold back your tender mercies from me. Let your unfailing love and faithfulness always protect me. For troubles surround me—too many to count!

PSALM 40:11-12

I took my troubles to the LORD; I cried out to him, and he answered my prayer. Rescue me, O LORD, from liars and from all deceitful people.

PSALM 120:1-2

Pecked by a hundred chickens

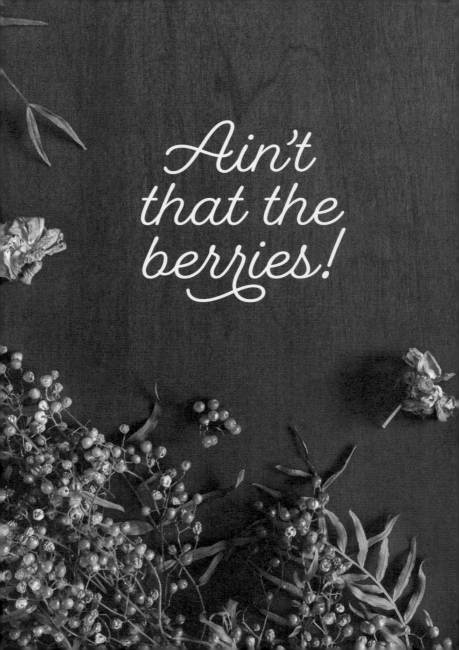

Ain't that the berries!

Expressing gratitude for God's goodness

Has it been a good few days for you? What positive things have come your way? Make note of everything you can think of. Then consider telling God, "Ain't that the berries!" So often we cry out to God when we're in the midst of troubles. We need to remember to express our thanks to him as well when life has given us berries and cream. But there's something more: The Bible not only tells us to thank the Lord when good things happen but also to praise his beautiful, glorious character. God *himself* is good! Spend some time thanking him for what he's done and for who he is.

Good and upright is the LORD; therefore he instructs sinners in his ways. He guides the humble in what is right and teaches them his way.

PSALM 25:8-9, NIV

Give thanks to the LORD, for he is good! His faithful love endures forever. Has the LORD redeemed you? Then speak out! Tell others he has redeemed you from your enemies.

PSALM 107:1-2

Dealing with pride

We see it in others—the turned-up noses, the snooty attitudes, the highfalutin language. Is there someone in your life these days who is like that? Are you thinking, *Who gave them the right to look down on me?* The Bible says they "wear pride like a jeweled necklace and clothe themselves with cruelty" (Psalm 73:6). That sounds exactly like a person who just got their second pair of britches. But there's another side to this coin: you. Is there someone in your life you look down on? Jesus said, "Why worry about a speck in your friend's eye when you have a log in your own?" (Matthew 7:3). Ask God to show you your own pairs of britches. Ask him to give you a heart filled with humility in your own life.

Do nothing out of selfish ambition or vain conceit. Rather, in humility value others above yourselves, not looking to your own interests but each of you to the interests of the others.

PHILIPPIANS 2:3-4, NIV

Some folks are
all right until
they get two pairs
of britches

Never give the
devil a ride—he'll
want the reins

Saying no to the enemy

It's no secret that the enemy of our souls wants to hijack our lives. An example of this is found in Luke 13, where Jesus encountered a woman who'd been crippled by an evil spirit. As a result, she spent much of her life "bent double" (Luke 13:11). Have you, too, been crippled? Has the devil taken the reins of your life? When Jesus saw the woman, "he called her over and said, 'Dear woman, you are healed of your sickness!' Then he touched her, and instantly she could stand straight" (Luke 13:12). The devil held her in bondage, but Jesus delivered her. Maybe you've given the enemy a ride in your life, or maybe he's taken the reins through the unfortunate actions of others. Either way, Jesus is here and wants to touch you with healing. Today, whatever your situation, say no to the devil and yes to Jesus.

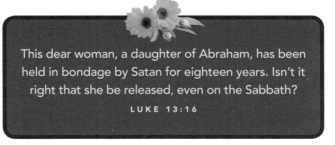

This dear woman, a daughter of Abraham, has been held in bondage by Satan for eighteen years. Isn't it right that she be released, even on the Sabbath?

LUKE 13:16

Trusting God for your everyday needs

Comedian Jeff Foxworthy said, "You might be a redneck if the Blue Book value of your truck goes up and down depending on how much gas it has in it." Does that sound like your vehicle? Maybe you feel so poor you couldn't jump over a nickel to save a dime. It's just difficult to make ends meet. Well, the Lord doesn't promise to make you wealthy, and you may still have to drive that ol' truck barely worth a plug nickel, but he *will* take care of you. Clean livin' is the key. When you make his business your business, he will supply all your needs.

Don't worry about these things, saying, "What will we eat? What will we drink? What will we wear?" These things dominate the thoughts of unbelievers, but your heavenly Father already knows all your needs. Seek the Kingdom of God above all else, and live righteously, and he will give you everything you need.

MATTHEW 6:31-33

So poor he had a tumbleweed as a pet

A half-truth
is a
whole lie

The real problem with not being real

These days, it's easy to use social media to present ourselves as someone we're not. We don't make up whole lies, of course, but sometimes we stretch the truth a little here, a little there. We create a view of ourselves that we want others to see. But the truth is, God made us and delights in us. As the apostle Paul said, "Before I was born, God chose me" (Galatians 1:15). So why shouldn't we be good and honest about who we are? After all, "honesty guides good people; dishonesty destroys treacherous people" (Proverbs 11:3). Seeking approval from others simply isn't an option when you're a child of God Most High. Enjoy the privilege of being true to yourself and to him.

Am I now seeking the approval of man, or of God? Or am I trying to please man? If I were still trying to please man, I would not be a servant of Christ.

GALATIANS 1:10, ESV

Don't lie to each other, for you have stripped off your old sinful nature and all its wicked deeds.

COLOSSIANS 3:9-10

Finding your top priority

Do you have so many to-do lists that you need a list of your lists to keep track of everything? Experts say that constant busyness isn't healthy; it hurts our relationships and leads to depression. The Bible adds one more truth: Busyness keeps us from the source of life—God himself. So here's an idea: Today, make one more list titled "What God Wants Me to Do." Write down what's most important to him, how he wants you to spend your time, and who the most important people in your life are. Let the priorities of your Master inform your master list.

[Martha] came to Jesus and said, "Lord, doesn't it seem unfair to you that my sister just sits here while I do all the work? Tell her to come and help me." But the Lord said to her, "My dear Martha, you are worried and upset over all these details! There is only one thing worth being concerned about. Mary has discovered it, and it will not be taken away from her."

LUKE 10:40-42

Busy as a stump-tailed cow in fly time

Stuck tighter than a hair in a biscuit

When you feel trapped by life

It's been a long, dry season, hasn't it? You've been longing for something different, something better, but it's always the same ol', same ol'. You're jammed tight. Sometimes we just need to wait for God's timing for us. We want what we want, but God has a better plan. Other times, though, our sin gets in the way of change, trapping us in a cycle that leaves us stuck tighter than a hair in a biscuit. If this is the case, maybe it's a good time for you to get with God. Confess what's holding you back. Then watch the Lord get you out of that rut!

Forget about what's happened; don't keep going over old history. Be alert, be present. I'm about to do something brand-new. It's bursting out! Don't you see it?

ISAIAH 43:18-19, MSG

Let us rid ourselves of everything that gets in the way, and of the sin which holds on to us so tightly, and let us run with determination the race that lies before us.

HEBREWS 12:1, GNT

Let go of the worries that weigh you down

Some people seem not to have a care in the world—they're always as happy as a dead pig in the sunshine. Are you one of them? Or do you collect your frets and fusses and let them keep you up at night? Jesus tells us not to worry about the frustrations of each day but to trust him for provision. Take your anxious thoughts to him and leave them at his feet. Jesus won't let you down . . . rest assured.

I tell you not to worry about everyday life—whether you have enough food and drink, or enough clothes to wear. Isn't life more than food, and your body more than clothing? Look at the birds. They don't plant or harvest or store food in barns, for your heavenly Father feeds them. And aren't you far more valuable to him than they are? Can all your worries add a single moment to your life?

MATTHEW 6:25-27

Give it to
God and
go to sleep

She's not God, but God has certainly been workin' through her

Pursuing God's own heart

We try so hard each day to accomplish everything that's on our plates. We want our affairs to run smoothly, after all. Yet while it's true that we need to git 'r done, our frantic efforts are often more about being in control. Some of us are playing God. You too? And how's that workin' out for you? You see, there's only one thing that matters. Ask yourself, *Is God revealing himself through my life?* He's looking for a few good women and men, people who pursue his heart. His heart is just and good—and most of all, filled with love. Will you commit your life today to God's purposes? Are you willing to let go and let him work through you? If so, you can be sure you'll have the strength you need.

The LORD has sought out a man after his own heart.

1 SAMUEL 13:14

The eyes of the LORD search the whole earth in order to strengthen those whose hearts are fully committed to him.

2 CHRONICLES 16:9

Belonging to God's family

In the Appalachians, a stranger might be asked, "Are you from off?" In other parts of the South, the question is, "Who are your people?" These questions simply reflect the importance of family to Southern folk. They also echo the beautiful story of Ruth in the Bible. Having lost her husband, Ruth chose to leave her country and go to Bethlehem with her mother-in-law, Naomi, who was returning to her own homeland in Israel. Ruth told Naomi, "Wherever you go, I will go; wherever you live, I will live. Your people will be my people, and your God will be my God" (Ruth 1:16). When a person decides to become a Christian, they, too, often choose a new family. These days, who are you hanging out with? Who are your people?

You Gentiles are no longer strangers and foreigners. You are citizens along with all of God's holy people. You are members of God's family. Together, we are his house, built on the foundation of the apostles and the prophets. And the cornerstone is Christ Jesus himself.

EPHESIANS 2:19-20

Who are your people?

Moving beyond acquaintances

There are people you know but don't *really* know, people you nod at in passing but somehow keep at a distance. For many, that's true of their relationship with Jesus. Is this your story too? Maybe you once said you were going to follow him, but now that's a distant memory. You and he—well, you howdied, but you never shook on the deal. Maybe it's time to move beyond acquaintances. Talk to him. Read his words to you in the Bible, and spend time with others who know him. Enjoy getting to know Jesus and making him the Lord of your life.

I will be their God, and they will be my people. And they will not need to teach their neighbors, nor will they need to teach their relatives, saying, "You should know the LORD." For everyone, from the least to the greatest, will know me already.

JEREMIAH 31:33-34

You must grow in the grace and knowledge of our Lord and Savior Jesus Christ. All glory to him, both now and forever!

2 PETER 3:18

Leading with a contagious passion

Don't ever apologize for your passion. Your love for Jesus is a beautiful thing. It springs from the work the Holy Spirit is doing in your heart. God did the same for Jesus' followers in the book of Acts: "What looked like flames or tongues of fire appeared and settled on each of them. And everyone present was filled with the Holy Spirit" (Acts 2:3-4). The Spirit has given you unique gifts that the world desperately needs, so don't let others dampen your passion! Your Savior has "overcome the world" (John 16:33)—and so can you. Ask God to stoke the beautiful holy fire that wonderfully rages inside you.

A deep sense of awe came over them all, and the apostles performed many miraculous signs and wonders.

ACTS 2:43

Do not quench the Spirit.

1 THESSALONIANS 5:19, NKJV

This girl's on fire!

Store the
Bible in your
heart, not on
a shelf

Reading God's Word
as part of your day

Do you ever think of reading the Bible as a chore that you put off because you don't really enjoy it? Yet the story it tells is the revelation of God himself. Why wouldn't you want to know what it says? The Bible speaks directly to you about who you are and the experiences life brings—your challenges and troubles, your joys and triumphs. Romans 15:4 says, "Even if it was written in Scripture long ago, you can be sure it's written for *us*" (MSG). So what are you waiting for? Dust off that Bible on your shelf and listen to God's words for you. As you soak in his truth and presence each day, the Bible will come alive in your heart.

Don't for a minute let this Book of The Revelation be out of mind. Ponder and meditate on it day and night, making sure you practice everything written in it. Then you'll get where you're going; then you'll succeed.

JOSHUA 1:8, MSG

Crying out to God

When was the last time everything in your life seemed to go wrong at once? Dealing with circumstances that are beyond what we can cope with leaves us feeling lower than a bowlegged caterpillar. In the Bible, King David often found himself overwhelmed and in the pit of despair. You can read many of his heartfelt pleas to God in the book of Psalms. His honesty shows us that it's okay to turn our goats loose, to yell to the high heavens and cry out to God from the depths of our hearts. Take courage: As the Lord did for David, he will do for you. For "Jesus Christ is the same yesterday, today, and forever" (Hebrews 13:8). Amen!

I waited patiently for the LORD to help me, and he turned to me and heard my cry. He lifted me out of the pit of despair, out of the mud and the mire. He set my feet on solid ground and steadied me as I walked along. He has given me a new song to sing, a hymn of praise to our God.

PSALM 40:1-3

Do your best,
and God will
do the rest

When success seems out of reach

You've worked hard for a long time. In every area of your life, you've kept after it, plodding on. But have there been setbacks, difficult circumstances, hardships that have made getting to the next level more challenging? Maybe people don't recognize your worth. Or perhaps you see success on the horizon, but it's still miles out of reach. Southern writer Fannie Flagg wrote, "Being a successful person is not necessarily defined by what you have achieved, but by what you have overcome." God doesn't look at what level you're at, and he knows the things you've had to overcome. He just wants you to stay close to him through prayer and reading his words of hope in the Bible. To God, that's real success. He'll do the rest.

Do your best to present yourself to God as one approved, a worker who does not need to be ashamed and who correctly handles the word of truth.

2 TIMOTHY 2:15, NIV

Pursuing a posture of prayer

Tiger Woods was the world's top golfer when his infidelity became public and his marriage crumbled. Later he reflected, "I convinced myself that normal rules did not apply. . . . I felt that I had worked hard my entire life and deserved to enjoy all the temptations around me." Maybe you've been feeling pretty peachy about yourself lately and think you deserve a little somethin' beyond the "normal rules." Listen to the warning of Scripture: "Be careful not to fall." In God's spiritual physics, the way we keep standing is by dropping to our knees. Assume a posture of prayer, give yourself humbly to God, and ask him to deliver you from sin's temptations.

If you think you are standing strong, be careful not to fall. The temptations in your life are no different from what others experience. And God is faithful. He will not allow the temptation to be more than you can stand. When you are tempted, he will show you a way out so that you can endure.

1 CORINTHIANS 10:12-13

A lot of kneelin' will keep you in good standin'

"I'll have
a coke"

Finding the language to communicate "the real thing"

If you walk into a restaurant in the Deep South and order a "coke," the server will ask, "What kind?" If you're a Yankee, you'll be confused. If you're a Southerner, you'll understand perfectly and reply, "Root beer" or "Make it a Mountain Dew" or, if you want *the real thing*, "Coca-Cola, please." In the South, "coke" means a soft drink of any kind. It's a fun reminder that some people use different language for certain things—even spiritual things. And that makes talking about Jesus a challenge. He's the real thing to you, but others might understand his name differently. Think about sharing your faith in a new way. Talk about how Jesus has changed your life, your thinking, your relationships. Let others taste the real Jesus, not just the brand name others know him by.

"What about you?" [Jesus] asked. "Who do you say I am?" Simon Peter answered, "You are the Messiah, the Son of the living God."

MATTHEW 16:15-16, NIV

The sin of gossip and meddling

No one who's a gossip admits to being one. Yet we all quickly point to someone who is. But that may be the pot calling the kettle black. It might be good to turn the mirror toward yourself. There's an age-old saying: "Gossip is saying behind someone's back what you would not say to their face. Flattery is saying to their face what you would not say behind their back." When put that way, how do you see yourself now? The Bible describes unrighteous people as "full of every kind of wickedness, sin, greed, hate, envy, murder, quarreling, deception, malicious behavior, and gossip" (Romans 1:29). Gossip is so hurtful and destructive that it makes God's top-ten evil traits list. So think about the potential of your words to damage or build up. Be kind and true in your talk *about* others and *to* others. And mind your own biscuits.

Do not spread slanderous gossip among your people.

LEVITICUS 19:16

A gossip goes around telling secrets, but those who are trustworthy can keep a confidence.

PROVERBS 11:13

Mind your
own biscuits,
and life will
be gravy

Glory be!

Amazed by God's handiwork

Remember those warm summer nights as a kid when you'd flop down on a patch of grass and simply stare at the night sky? The wonder of stars and planets and the beauty of God's creation filled you. As an adult you've probably been missing out on those experiences. You never seem to have time, do you? Maybe it's time to make time. Do you know a place where you can surround yourself with God's incredible creation? Perhaps the crest of a mountain, the bank of a river, an open place in the woods, your own backyard? Why not seek that out? Make an appointment to stare at the handiwork of God. Let yourself be amazed by him; it's good for the soul. Glory be!

LORD, our Lord, how majestic is your name in all the earth! . . . When I consider your heavens, the work of your fingers, the moon and the stars, which you have set in place, what is mankind that you are mindful of them, human beings that you care for them?

PSALM 8:1, 3-4, NIV

Getting the most out of life

Are you a planner, or do you just go with the flow? If you're like most people, you'd probably say a mix of the two. What about the day ahead of you? Will you just roll with it and let life happen around you? Or will you make it as delicious as it can be, drinking in the sweet juice God has for you? Matthew 5:6 says, "You're blessed when you've worked up a good appetite for God. He's food and drink in the best meal you'll ever eat" (MSG). As you tackle your to-do list, seek God by thirsting for what he has for you. Squeeze the day for all it's worth and find quenching joy in his perfect plan.

You will show me the way of life, granting me the joy of your presence and the pleasures of living with you forever.

PSALM 16:11

Squeeze
the day

Worn slap out

When you're exhausted by life

Is this a perfect description for how you feel right now? Maybe it's from the demands of work or the challenge of taking care of children. Maybe it's for lack of sleep, your worries keeping you up at night. Whatever the reason, you find yourself exhausted, just worn slap out. Of course, correcting the problem isn't always easy, but perhaps you can take some comfort from knowing that Jesus, too, got tired. Once when he was amid multitudes of people clamoring to see him, he said to his disciples, "Let's go off by ourselves to a quiet place and rest awhile" (Mark 6:31). Think of his statement as an invitation to you as well. Do what you can to spend some time in a quiet place with Jesus. Even if you don't sleep, you will enter into his rest and receive his comfort.

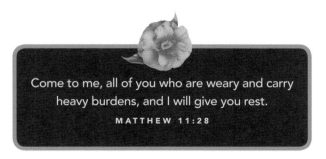

Come to me, all of you who are weary and carry heavy burdens, and I will give you rest.

MATTHEW 11:28

Riding into your day with courage

Watching the Kentucky Derby leaves no question about the sheer strength, power, and breathtaking beauty of a thoroughbred. The Bible speaks of how God gave the horse its "prowess" and how it "laughs at danger, fearless," and "doesn't shy away from the sword" (Job 39:19, 22, MSG). Perhaps this week you've been beaten down. Why not approach the day ahead as though you were perched in the saddle of a mighty white horse? Why not ride into your world with courage? Know that God arms you with strength. He will enable you to jump over your obstacles, race ahead of your problems, and gallop into the fray with confidence, courage, and oh-so-glorious overcoming power.

Who is God except the LORD? Who but our God is a solid rock? God arms me with strength, and he makes my way perfect.

PSALM 18:31-32

God has come to save me. I will trust in him and not be afraid. The LORD GOD is my strength and my song; he has given me victory.

ISAIAH 12:2

Raised on
God and
horses

Too blessed
to be
stressed

Count your best things

Sometimes it's really true: When it rains it pours. When stress descends on you all at once, it can become a real toad-strangler of a week (or month . . . or year). To boot, the things that are stressing you might be depressing you. Maybe that's where you find yourself right now. Well, the Bible has some simple advice: Make a list of the best things in your life and focus on them. Remember how God has come through for you in the past. Thank him for that then, and trust him in this now. You're too blessed to be stressed!

Do not be anxious about anything, but in every situation, by prayer and petition, with thanksgiving, present your requests to God. . . . Whatever is true, whatever is noble, whatever is right, whatever is pure, whatever is lovely, whatever is admirable—if anything is excellent or praiseworthy—think about such things.

PHILIPPIANS 4:6, 8, NIV

Filling your life with the One who saves

It's good to start your morning with a fresh, warm biscuit and a steaming cup of coffee as you watch the early sun spread into the sky. But that's not all that's good. After filling up your tummy, take time to bask in the presence of the One who brings salvation. Read some Scripture and talk to Jesus in prayer. Filling yourself up with his presence will always make your day. Psalm 90:14 says, "Satisfy us each morning with your unfailing love, so we may sing for joy," and Job 23:12 says, "I have not departed from his commands, but have treasured his words more than daily food." The evidence is overwhelming: All you need is a little bit of coffee (okay—throw in a biscuit, too) and a whole lot of Jesus!

Listen to my voice in the morning, Lord. Each morning
I bring my requests to you and wait expectantly.

PSALM 5:3

Rising very early in the morning, while it was still dark, [Jesus]
departed and went out to a desolate place, and there he prayed.

MARK 1:35, ESV

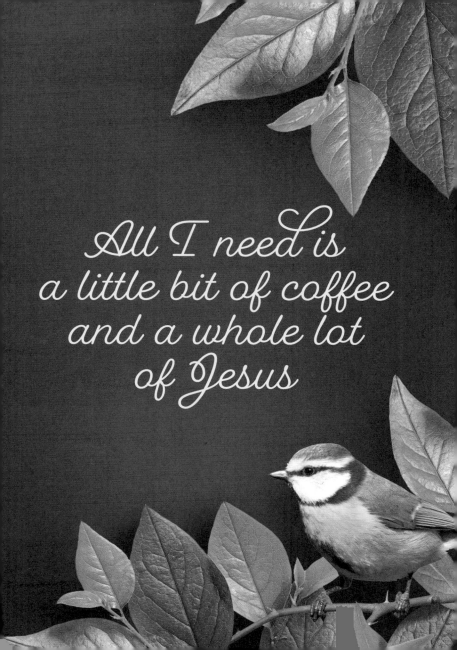

You can't tell how deep a well is by measurin' the length of the pump handle

Looks can be deceiving

We live in a time when it's hard to know what's real and what's fake. Someone or something that looks beautiful might in fact be some kind of ugly in disguise. Those who look like sheep may actually be wolves. What are you to do about the fakers around you? The Bible says to look at their fruit—in other words, to examine the results of their actions. And as you do, perhaps look at yourself in the mirror. Are you presenting yourself as someone you're not? What is the fruit of your life? Ask God to protect you from deception—from others and from within.

Beware of false prophets who come disguised as harmless sheep but are really vicious wolves. You can identify them by their fruit, that is, by the way they act.

MATTHEW 7:15-16

Do not be deceived: God cannot be mocked. A man reaps what he sows. Whoever sows to please their flesh, from the flesh will reap destruction; whoever sows to please the Spirit, from the Spirit will reap eternal life.

GALATIANS 6:7-8, NIV

Nowhere to run, nowhere to hide

A boy ran by a man standing on the curb. Five minutes later, the boy ran by again. The third time, the boy yelled to the man, "I'm running away from home!" The man said, "But you've only gone around the block. It's been three times now." The boy answered, "I know. My mom won't let me cross the street." You know, it's funny how we tend to run in circles. But even when we do, God is watching over us to make sure we don't run too far. Maybe you're still running from your mother or father. Maybe you're running from a relationship that got difficult. Or maybe you're running from God. The truth is that Jesus loves you anyway. Can you hear him calling you home?

Nothing can ever separate us from God's love. . . . No power in the sky above or in the earth below—indeed, nothing in all creation will ever be able to separate us from the love of God that is revealed in Christ Jesus our Lord.

ROMANS 8:38-39

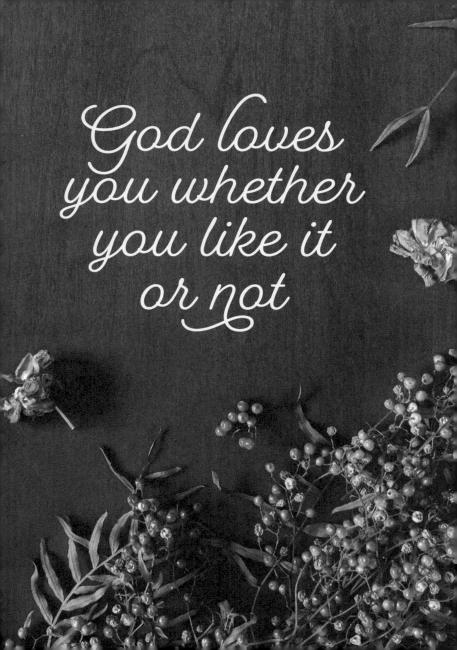

Don't tell God how big your problem is. Tell your problem how big God is!

Move that mountain

It may be that you've made a molehill into a mountain. Or perhaps your problem truly is big and bothering. Either way, it feels as huge as Georgia, and you don't see any way of solving it or changing your situation. Of course, it's always best to take these things to God in prayer, but there's also wisdom in giving your problem a talkin'-to. You might just want to tell your mountain (or molehill) how big and powerful your God is. See if all the fears and worries that make up your mound don't just start to crumble away.

In his presence the mountains quake, and the hills melt away; the earth trembles.

NAHUM 1:5

"You don't have enough faith," Jesus told them. "I tell you the truth, if you had faith even as small as a mustard seed, you could say to this mountain, 'Move from here to there,' and it would move. Nothing would be impossible."

MATTHEW 17:20-21

"Do unto others . . ."

If you tell a Northerner you're helping a friend "make groceries" at the Piggly Wiggly, they would probably laugh or give you a clueless look. Of course, you don't mean you're cooking up dinner for your best bud. No, you're helping them shop at the grocery store! But here's the bigger picture: When you assist others with their needs, Jesus said it's the same as serving him: "As you did it to one of the least of these my brothers, you did it to me" (Matthew 25:40, ESV). Whom might you help today?

Suppose you see a brother or sister who has no food or clothing, and you say, "Good-bye and have a good day; stay warm and eat well"—but then you don't give that person any food or clothing. What good does that do? So you see, faith by itself isn't enough. Unless it produces good deeds, it is dead and useless.

JAMES 2:15-17

Makin' groceries

Finding your passion in life

Today as you head to work or stop at the Dollar General or make groceries at Walmart, think about the things in life that bring you excitement. Your best passion is something that energizes you, has meaning beyond yourself, and leaves a lasting impact. What tugs at your heart, gets you going in the morning, cranks your tractor? A tip: Your best passion is also something that makes God smile. God's "plan for your life" may actually be many things at different times, but it's always a path that you and he walk together. With that in mind, in this season of your life, what is your passion? Ask the Lord for more opportunities to serve him in this important and inspiring way.

Jesus said, "The first [commandment] in importance is . . .
'Love the Lord God with all your passion and prayer
and intelligence and energy.' And here is the second:
'Love others as well as you love yourself.' There is no
other commandment that ranks with these."

MARK 12:29-31, msg

Receive power to overcome

Do you ever feel like you're drowning in "You're not . . ."
messages? *You're not beautiful. You're not intelligent. You're not capable.*
Has the world planted those lies in your mind? It's enough to
make a country girl mad. But instead of stewing in your anger,
go to God's Word and reclaim the truth of his "You are . . ."
messages: "You are altogether beautiful, my darling, beautiful
in every way," says Song of Songs 4:7. The Bible also says you
are "fearfully and wonderfully made" (Psalm 139:14, NIV) and
that God has not given you "a spirit of fear and timidity, but
of power, love, and self-discipline" (2 Timothy 1:7). Embrace
the promises of God. Receive his power to become the strong
woman he had in mind when he created you. After all, that
backhoe's a-waitin'.

She is clothed with strength and dignity, and she laughs
without fear of the future. When she speaks, her words
are wise, and she gives instructions with kindness.

PROVERBS 31:25-26

Never anger a
country girl who
can run a backhoe

Your
bestest
friend

Praying with the one you're closest to

Comedienne Jeanne Robertson likes to explain how Southern women have best friends and "bestest" friends. The joke is that almost everyone is a Southern woman's best friend—even someone she's just met. But a *bestest* friend is one you trust to tell the truth about yourself. Robertson says it's like when you're going somewhere important. You finish your makeup and get in the car looking your very finest. Your bestest friend looks at your face closely and says, "You missed your mouth." In spiritual terms, a bestest friend is also someone you can pray with. So who is your bestest friend, the one who cares enough to tell you the truth about yourself? Will you trust her enough to pray together?

Wounds from a sincere friend are better
than many kisses from an enemy.

PROVERBS 27:6

If two of you agree here on earth concerning anything you ask,
my Father in heaven will do it for you. For where two or three
gather together as my followers, I am there among them.

MATTHEW 18:19-20

Sometimes we cry

Country singer Chris Stapleton's song "Sometimes I Cry" is about a lost love, although its sentiment could apply to so many of the losses we experience in our lives. And although "nothin' dries as quick as a tear" means that feelings usually pass quickly, sometimes we just can't move on. Sometimes we just keep crying. Maybe this is where you are in your life right now. What or whom are your tears shed for? God doesn't guarantee that we'll escape from pain in this world. He doesn't promise we'll only cry a few tears. But he does offer water for our souls and comfort in him. Have you ever shared your tears with him?

They will never again be hungry or thirsty; they will never be scorched by the heat of the sun. For the Lamb on the throne will be their Shepherd. He will lead them to springs of life-giving water. And God will wipe every tear from their eyes.

REVELATION 7:16-17

Nothin' dries
as quick as
a tear

I'm goin'
by your
house later

Stopping in instead of driving by

If you're not from Louisiana, you might misunderstand when a friend tells you, "I'm goin' by your house later." *Okay,* you think, *but she doesn't need to tell me that she's just driving by.* But in the state of Cajun and Creole, "goin' by your house" means she's aimin' to stop in for a visit and spend time with you. Maybe there's a spiritual tip in this. In your relationship with Jesus, are you just driving by or stopping in? Maybe recently you've sped right past having some good visiting time with him. Don't forget how extraordinary it is that through Jesus, we have access to God's presence. How about goin' by his house later?

We are made fit for God by the once-for-all sacrifice of Jesus. . . . So, friends, we can now—without hesitation— walk right up to God, into "the Holy Place.". . . So let's *do* it— full of belief, confident that we're presentable inside and out. Let's keep a firm grip on the promises that keep us going.

HEBREWS 10:10, 19, 22, MSG

Healing from heartbreak

Can you remember wanting something very badly when you were a kid? Do you recall your disappointment when you didn't get it? Or maybe your first crush, someone you liked very much, didn't feel the same way about you—and it still stings today. Life is filled with disappointments. Even as you get older, your wants can end up hurting you. Perhaps this is the season of life you're in now. But now that you're wiser, turn to God for comfort instead. He doesn't promise you freedom from the pain of denial, but he does offer you himself. He is enough. Center yourself in him and let him be the desire of your heart.

Trust in the LORD, and do good; dwell in the land and befriend faithfulness. Delight yourself in the LORD, and he will give you the desires of your heart.

PSALM 37:3-4, ESV

He heals the brokenhearted and binds up their wounds.

PSALM 147:3, NKJV

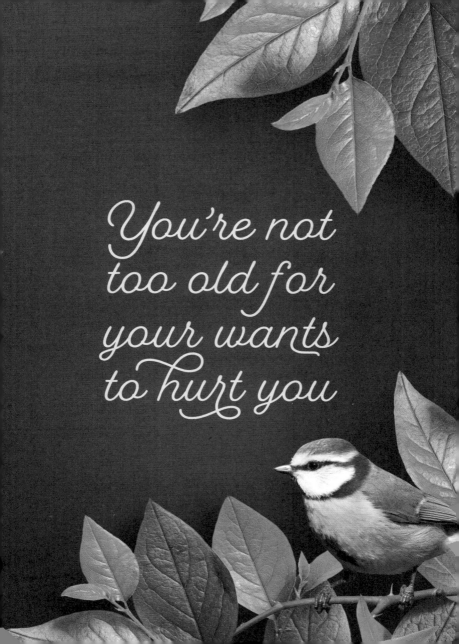

Goodness
gracious,
sakes alive!

Praising God's character

"Goodness gracious, sakes alive!" Probably those who say this don't know what it really means. But it might be a good thing to say, and to say often. See, this expression praises the very personality of God himself. You might think that God is severe and unforgiving, but the Bible says he is *gracious* and full of *goodness*. You might think you're stuck in God's doghouse, but the Bible says he wants to forgive you and embrace you. Jesus is all about goodness and graciousness, and for our sake, he is alive indeed! "The One who died for us—who was raised to life for us!—is in the presence of God at this very moment sticking up for us" (Romans 8:34, MSG). Take time today to thank God for his gracious goodness and love for you.

The LORD, the LORD God, merciful and gracious, longsuffering, and abounding in goodness and truth, keeping mercy for thousands, forgiving iniquity and transgression and sin.

EXODUS 34:6-7, NKJV

Take a deep breath

Has your life gone crazier than a betsy bug? "Slow your roll" likely captures the perfect advice for you during this frantic time: Let go. Relax. Take a breath when you're beside yourself. The Bible says to "quiet down before GOD, be prayerful before him" (Psalm 37:7, MSG). Spend some time with the Lord while you enjoy the beauty in the evening sky he painted or listen to his symphony in the chatter of cricket sounds. In him alone will you find true and lasting rest, so let him quiet your heart and slow your roll.

Be still, and know that I am God; I will be exalted among the nations, I will be exalted in the earth! The LORD of hosts is with us; the God of Jacob is our refuge.

PSALM 46:10-11, NKJV

Slow down. Take a deep breath. What's the hurry? Why wear yourself out? Just what are you after anyway?

JEREMIAH 2:25, MSG

Don't go borrowin' trouble

Live for today and trust for tomorrow

If your grandma ever told you, "Don't go borrowin' trouble," she meant that worrying about tomorrow is taking on more than you need to. It's interesting that the Bible uses the phrases "do not worry" or "do not fear" many times. Seems that people in Bible times were like we are today. Are you constantly fretting about what will happen later this week, in another month, or even next year? Maybe it's time you let go of worrying about the future—and remember to trust in the Lord. Focus on Jesus and his promises right now, today, and don't go borrowin' trouble from tomorrow.

Give your entire attention to what God is doing right now, and don't get worked up about what may or may not happen tomorrow. God will help you deal with whatever hard things come up when the time comes.

MATTHEW 6:34, MSG

Give all your worries and cares to God, for he cares about you.

1 PETER 5:7

How's it goin'?

"How's it goin'?" people often ask. "Just fine," we say without thinking, whether we're fine or not. But sometimes it's good to actually take stock and ask ourselves how we're doing in life. After listing your problems and needs, take some time to focus on all that God has provided. Think about the talents and abilities he's given you. Ponder the people who bring you joy. Of course, since he *is* God, he already knows how you're doin', but he would love for you to talk to him about it. Perhaps you might tell him, "I'm pretty good, thanks to you. Fine as frog hair and not half as slick."

God is able to bless you abundantly, so that in all things at all times, having all that you need, you will abound in every good work.

2 CORINTHIANS 9:8, NIV

I have learned how to be content with whatever I have. I know how to live on almost nothing or with everything. I have learned the secret of living in every situation, whether it is with a full stomach or empty, with plenty or little.

PHILIPPIANS 4:11-12

I'm fine
as frog hair
and not half
as slick

Staying true to yourself

It seems there's always someone else we wish we could be: that girl who has achieved great things, looks a certain way, is living the life we want. Who is that person in your life? It's not wrong to have a role model, but in aiming to be like another, we might stop being ourselves. What if you were to live wide open as a Case knife—comfortable just being yourself and letting others see what you have to offer? Our good God wants you to be you—the person he's shaping to be like him in *character* but with all the wonderful personality traits that he created in you *specifically*. As "God's masterpiece" (Ephesians 2:10), enjoy the freedom he offers to find your true self in him, not in someone else.

You formed my inward parts; you knitted me together in my mother's womb.

PSALM 139:13, ESV

God knew his people in advance, and he chose them to become like his Son, so that his Son would be the firstborn among many brothers and sisters.

ROMANS 8:29

Appreciating the best things in life

Jesus asked her to fetch him a drink of water. They sat at a well where the water was plentiful, yet her life was dry. Dry as a barn full of sawdust. Are you living in a dry season of life right now? Are you thirsty for fresh life? For the woman at the well, the best surprise of her entire life was sitting right there. Jesus told her, "If you only knew the gift God has for you and who you are speaking to, you would ask me, and I would give you living water" (John 4:10). Perhaps you know Jesus but have forgotten that only he can satisfy your thirst. Or maybe you've never known him, not really. Come to Jesus now. Ask him to pour you a never-ending cup of his living water.

Those who drink the water I give will never be thirsty again. It becomes a fresh, bubbling spring within them, giving them eternal life.

JOHN 4:14

A dry well teaches us the worth of water

Quit wishing and get busy

Back in the day, you could get anything from the Sears catalog, even farm machinery. Maybe you remember leafing through their Christmas catalog, called *The Wish Book*, when you were a kid. Filled with pictures of toys and games, you'd call dibs on each treasure you wanted. You've outgrown that, of course, but maybe you still spend lots of time exercising your wishing muscles. Sometimes you long for more things and want your life to be different. Are you sitting in a self-pity party of wish making? That's not what God wants. He's calling you to be a person who gives from the abundance of what you've received. Change your wishing well by acting, not sitting. Thank God for all he has given you, and pray about how you can give to others.

> I am praying that you will put into action the generosity that comes from your faith as you understand and experience all the good things we have in Christ.
>
> **PHILEMON 1:6**

The pleasure of walking with Jesus

Country legend Hank Williams wrote the song "Are You Walking and A-Talking for the Lord?" It poses questions about our deeds as we journey along life's highway. Are we "being Jesus" to others who need him? Are we walking with him each day despite hardships? Unfortunately, because we so easily misunderstand what happiness truly is, we're inclined to seek superficial, temporary pleasures. Have a talk with yourself and the Lord. Discover the lasting joy that can only be found in sharing your journey with him.

You shall walk in all the way that the LORD your God has commanded you, that you may live, and that it may go well with you, and that you may live long in the land that you shall possess.

DEUTERONOMY 5:33, ESV

God blesses those who patiently endure testing and temptation. Afterward they will receive the crown of life that God has promised to those who love him.

JAMES 1:12

Happiness is in heaven, but joy is in the journey

She's not
from around
here, is she?

Living different from the world

The Christian life isn't easy because following Jesus sets you apart from those around you—sometimes even friends and family. When they don't share your beliefs, they're likely to see you as an alien in their ordinary world. Of course, it's hard to be judged that way, and you might be tempted to fit in by sacrificing your values. But remember what Jesus said: "If the world hates you, keep in mind that it hated me first" (John 15:18, NIV). He is "the living bread that came down from heaven" (John 6:51). See, as one who embraces Jesus, you really aren't from around here, are you?

If you belonged to the world, it would love you as its own. As it is, you do not belong to the world, but I have chosen you out of the world. That is why the world hates you.

JOHN 15:19, NIV

We are citizens of heaven, where the Lord Jesus Christ lives. And we are eagerly waiting for him to return as our Savior.

PHILIPPIANS 3:20

Embracing the hard times

One time-honored Southern tradition is making pickles. Just a few ingredients change a cucumber spear into a deliciously sweet and tangy pickle. But there is one ingredient that is most essential: vinegar. It's the acid in vinegar that changes the cucumber in just the right way to give it the flavor that makes it a favorite. Likewise, God uses the vinegar of life's trials to make us "perfect and complete" (James 1:4). As you try to make sense of some of the sourness in your life right now, take some time in prayer to thank God for transforming you into a person of sweetness, tang, and flavor who is his perfect delight.

We can rejoice, too, when we run into problems and trials, for we know that they help us develop endurance. And endurance develops strength of character, and character strengthens our confident hope of salvation. And this hope will not lead to disappointment. For we know how dearly God loves us, because he has given us the Holy Spirit to fill our hearts with his love.

ROMANS 5:3-5

I'm gonna jerk a knot in your tail!

The upside of discipline

I'm gonna jerk a knot in your tail! Did a parent or an authority figure ever invoke this colorful phrase on you while you were growing up? Despite its heavy-handed imagery, it only means that if you don't straighten up, discipline will follow. Have you found this happening to you as an adult today? You're speeding along chasing something you think you want when suddenly a mysterious force stops you cold in your tracks. If you look back, you might find the Lord holding your "tail." The good news is that God doesn't discipline you to harm you but to make you better. "The LORD disciplines those he loves." Maybe he's protecting you. Maybe he's keeping you from doing wrong. Or maybe he's telling you to take a different road. What's God saying to you today?

My child, don't make light of the LORD's discipline, and don't give up when he corrects you. For the LORD disciplines those he loves, and he punishes each one he accepts as his child.

HEBREWS 12:5-6

Getting beyond the mess

So you've made a mess of things. Maybe you did something wrong, then tried to "fix" it by doing something else you shouldn't have, or maybe by telling a lie. Now you're knee-deep in greasy black okra. Remember, the Bible says we've all messed up. That doesn't get you out of the frying pan, but there is another path. God says that if you confess your sins to him, he'll help you. Perhaps there are also others you need to confess to. You can't control how people will respond, but chances are they'll respect you for owning up. You *do* know how God will respond. He'll not only forgive you but also make something beautiful out of your mess. You can count on him.

We know that God causes everything to work together for the good of those who love God and are called according to his purpose for them.

ROMANS 8:28

If we confess our sins, he who is faithful and just will forgive us our sins and cleanse us from all unrighteousness.

1 JOHN 1:9, NRSV

Worse than
burnt okra
stuck to
the pan

What in
tarnation?!

The mind-boggling gift of salvation

What in tarnation?! Rural folk often use this phrase when they're surprised by something that's mind-boggling. The word *tarnation* has an interesting origin. Around the late 1700s, people started combining two words—*eternal* and *darnation* (that's a nicer word for . . . well, you can probably guess). The Bible has a lot to say about both. We all have a sin problem that destines us for eternal punishment—that is, until we follow Jesus. When we commit ourselves to him, we're assured of eternal life and receive his Holy Spirit so we can live good, clean lives. God living with us is mind-boggling indeed! The next time you hear this phrase, say a word of thanks to Jesus and remember the extraordinary story of what he did for you.

Everyone has sinned; we all fall short of God's glorious standard. Yet God, in his grace, freely makes us right in his sight. He did this through Christ Jesus when he freed us from the penalty for our sins.

ROMANS 3:23-24

Overcoming spiritual dryness

How dry and dusty is your life these days? How long has it been since you enjoyed spiritual refreshment? Maybe it seems God is silent or—worse yet—has even forsaken you. Maybe your prayers have gone unanswered. The psalmist David felt that way, too, when he said, "My God, my God, why have you abandoned me? . . . Every night I lift my voice, but I find no relief" (Psalm 22:1-2). Yet the truth is that God always shows up in his perfect timing. David also testified, "You sent abundant rain, O God, to refresh the weary land. . . . You provided for your needy people" (Psalm 68:9-10). So don't be afraid to stay the course. Wait upon the Lord, and continue to pray. God is faithful. He will provide the living water you so desperately need!

Anyone who is thirsty may come to me! Anyone who believes in me may come and drink! For the Scriptures declare, "Rivers of living water will flow from his heart."

JOHN 7:37-38

It's so dry
the trees
are bribin'
the dogs

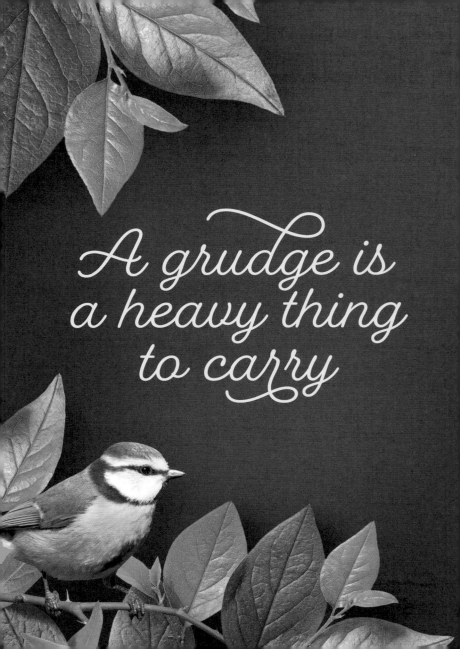

A grudge is
a heavy thing
to carry

The poison of resentment

Is there someone in your life you hold something against? A resentment, perhaps going way back? Maybe the grudge you hold has never been addressed. And maybe this person actually *did* do wrong. Yet this grudge hurts only you. Someone once said, "Resentment is like swallowing poison and waiting for the other person to die." God forbids holding grudges because he knows they eat away at us from the inside. Take your issue to the Lord and release the burden to him. Then follow his lead about going to this person in love and forgiveness. You'll feel much lighter—guaranteed.

Don't seek revenge or carry a grudge against any of your people. Love your neighbor as yourself. I am GOD.

LEVITICUS 19:18, MSG

Get rid of all bitterness, rage, anger, harsh words, and slander, as well as all types of evil behavior. Instead, be kind to each other, tenderhearted, forgiving one another, just as God through Christ has forgiven you.

EPHESIANS 4:31-32

Reclaim the pleasures of the Christian life

The rumor going around is that the Christian life is full of rules. Maybe you're in a valley right now, a place where joy and pleasure are nowhere to be seen. Everything feels like a have-to. But Jesus said, "My purpose is to give [my people] a rich and satisfying life" (John 10:10). Far from being a killjoy, God wants you chock-full of blessings. The problem is that we often think in terms of material things. Yet God says our only true joy comes from relationships—relationships with others and especially a relationship with God himself. Remove your focus from what you don't have, and gaze upon the God who loves you without limit. Lift your eyes from the valley and find God on the mountaintop.

I have told you these things so that you will be filled with my joy. Yes, your joy will overflow! This is my commandment: Love each other in the same way I have loved you.

JOHN 15:11-12

If you have no joy,
there's a leak in your
faith somewhere

And how!

Consider all that God has done

"It's hotter'n blue blazes," someone says. It really *is* hotter than Georgia asphalt. You reach for your iced tea and put in your vote of agreement. "And how!" you reply. That simple phrase usually refers to something that was already said or done and adds an exclamation point. It looks back. It's your hearty nod to something in the past. Well, maybe as you step into your day ahead, you might think about all the things God has done for you lately: How he worked out a problem you were struggling with. How he answered your prayer yesterday. How he helped you through a health issue. Maybe it's time for you to say, "Amen!" for all he has previously done. Or perhaps you prefer to praise him for his amazing work in your life by shouting out a hearty, "And how!"

Stop and consider the wonderful miracles of God!

JOB 37:14

The greatest love story ever told

In the classic 1939 movie *Gone with the Wind*, Rhett Butler declares to Scarlett O'Hara, "I love you more than I've ever loved any woman. And I've waited longer for you than I've ever waited for any woman." The greatest love story of all time, though, is God's love for the world. Jesus *died* to give you eternal life—because he loves you so very much—and he waits patiently for you to run into his arms. Today, take time to leaf through the photo album of your mind and recall the many times God showed his deep love for you. As you reflect on all that he's done, let it compel you to live more fully for him.

May you have the power to understand, as all God's people should, how wide, how long, how high, and how deep his love is. May you experience the love of Christ, though it is too great to understand fully. Then you will be made complete with all the fullness of life and power that comes from God.

EPHESIANS 3:18-19

God
love her

An empty
bucket
makes the
most racket

See through the guise

Is there someone in your life who is persuasive with the in-crowd or dominates at social events? A person who makes herself the center of attention often does so out of insecurity and a pre-occupation with appearances. Yet those who talk the most often have the least to say. Proverbs 10:19 teaches, "The more talk, the less truth" (MSG). The Bible warns against being taken in by shallow, immature people, so make an effort to see through the guise. Pray they'll find their identity in the Lord and not in a popularity contest. In the meantime, focus on becoming the person of godly character that God wants you to be.

These are the gifts Christ gave to the church: the apostles, the prophets, the evangelists, and the pastors and teachers. Their responsibility is to equip God's people to do his work and build up the church. . . . Then we will no longer be immature like children. . . . We will not be influenced when people try to trick us with lies so clever they sound like the truth.

EPHESIANS 4:11-12, 14

Help for breaking unhealthy habits

At one time it was thought the phrase "quittin' cold turkey" surfaced because addicts going through withdrawal sometimes developed goose bumps and pale, translucent skin, like a plucked turkey. In any case, "quittin' cold turkey" doesn't apply only to addiction. It can be about leaving behind any number of things we feel a need to indulge in repeatedly. What habits do you need to quit cold turkey? Can you identify any obsessions that have taken over your time and replaced the Lord as your top priority? Giving up those things is hard, but this is serious stuff. Talk to your heavenly Father about it. Confess your shortcomings and ask him for motivation to make things right. With help from God and others, you can live a balanced, healthy life.

Throw off your old sinful nature and your former way of life, which is corrupted by lust and deception. Instead, let the Spirit renew your thoughts and attitudes.

EPHESIANS 4:22-23

I can do everything through Christ, who gives me strength.

PHILIPPIANS 4:13

Quittin'
cold turkey

Give your Troubles
to God—he'll be up
all night anyhow

Resting easy

Why is it that when we camped as kids, we loved to tell scary stories? Around a campfire deep in the woods, someone would spin the tale of an escaped convict or a monster bear, and we'd be up all night imagining that some sound we heard was the outlaw sneaking up on us or the bear scraping the side of our tents. As an adult, you don't need to imagine troubles—you have real worries all your own. Maybe they're even keeping you up at night. But what if you were to bring your troubles to God before you go to bed? Try laying them at his feet in prayer. The Bible says the Lord "never slumbers or sleeps" (Psalm 121:4). He's like a lookout watching the camp during the night. He's got you covered. Rest easy.

Give your worries to the LORD, and he will take care of you.

PSALM 55:22, NCV

Asking for help in times of trouble

Maybe the news you got recently was really hard to take, perhaps another discouragement in a year full of setbacks. Or maybe it was something more serious that felt like a gut punch. Have circumstances hit you hard? The Bible tells how the apostle Paul was imprisoned and beaten many times—persecuted for telling others the Good News about Jesus. Yet he turned to God in his deepest troubles, praising him and praying for the needs around him. Paul even wrote to his fellow Christians, encouraging them to "rejoice in . . . confident hope" (Romans 12:12). When life has driven you down, stay on your knees and turn your problems into prayers. Take your troubles to God and let him whisper to you in your hardest times. "Then you will experience God's peace, which exceeds anything we can understand" (Philippians 4:7).

Be patient in trouble, and keep on praying.

ROMANS 12:12

When life
knocks you on
your knees,
you're in a perfect
position to pray

Sittin' below
the salt

When you lose your standing

Ever feel like you've lost your place in the world? Maybe you didn't get that promotion at work you were hoping for, or perhaps you feel abandoned by a friend or family member. The old saying is that you're "sittin' below the salt," not moving up in social rank or recognition. It's disappointing, sure. But you know, it doesn't matter in the big scheme of things. Jesus said that God blesses those who realize their need for him; they're the ones who will inherit the fullness of his Kingdom. There is no greater promotion, no greater standing than what you already possess in God's esteem. Take a moment to let go of your expectations. Thank the Lord for giving you the most important position of all—a place in his Kingdom.

Blessed are the poor in spirit, for theirs is the kingdom of heaven. . . . Blessed are the meek, for they shall inherit the earth.

MATTHEW 5:3, 5, ESV

Walking with God through life's endings

Sometimes it's just hard to let go of certain things in your life. Can you relate? Maybe you struggle with a bad habit or practice. Perhaps you're caught in an abusive relationship. Or it might be that you're pining for someone who is no longer in your life—for a good reason. What are you still holding on to? If God has clearly whispered to you that he wants you to end it, have you resisted by making his "Stop" into your "Maybe"? It's always helpful to share your question marks with Jesus. Don't be afraid to tell him why it's hard for you to put a period on this issue. He understands your struggle and wants to help. Will you trust him?

Trust in the LORD with all your heart and lean not on your own understanding; in all your ways submit to him, and he will make your paths straight. Do not be wise in your own eyes; fear the LORD and shun evil.

PROVERBS 3:5-7, NIV

Don't put a
question mark
where God
put a period

She's as
honest as the
day is long

Becoming a person of truth

Mrs. Threadgoode, in Fannie Flagg's novel *Fried Green Tomatoes at the Whistle Stop Cafe*, says, "You never know what's in a person's heart until they're tested, do you?" Often our hearts harbor good intentions but deceiving methods. It feels easier to be slippery with the truth. Doing so helps us skate past difficult conversations—at least in the hurry of the moment. And under the glare of accusations, it helps us slide around admissions of failure. The problem is that at some point we are tested, exposing our deceptions to others. Maybe it's time to try an experiment: Ask God to help you become a person of complete truth. Over time, people will come to respect your integrity and honesty. And most important, you'll feel God's smile upon your transformation.

People with integrity walk safely, but those who follow crooked paths will be exposed.

PROVERBS 10:9

Stop telling lies. Let us tell our neighbors the truth, for we are all parts of the same body.

EPHESIANS 4:25

Working hard in God's fields

Did you hear about the employee who was caught asleep at work, his head resting on his keyboard? When he was roused, he quickly explained, "I was just testing it for drool resistance." Of course, there's no question that *you* work hard; you have no fear of good, honest sweat. But maybe the bigger question is, What work are you doing for Jesus? How are you laboring to bring his Kingdom to earth? This important task isn't restricted to our day jobs; it's anything we do to share God's love and sow the seed of his Word in people's hearts. What is that opportunity for you?

The harvest is great, but the workers are few. So pray to the Lord who is in charge of the harvest; ask him to send more workers into his fields.

MATTHEW 9:37-38

The one who plants and the one who waters work together with the same purpose. And both will be rewarded for their own hard work.

1 CORINTHIANS 3:8

Nobody
ever drowned
in sweat

Relinquishing your grip

When Appalachian folk say "Let all holds go," they mean you should put everything aside to do the one thing in front of you. It has rich meaning in our everyday lives as well as our spiritual lives. To focus on Jesus each day, we need to "let all holds go"— to relinquish what we're holding on to. And maybe you know from your own experience that's not so easy. The things we hold close and dear are often things we worship with our time and attention. Do you have idols like these that you are holding tight? Tell Jesus you need help letting all holds go. He's eager to spend time with you!

Sacrifices offered to idols are offered to nothing,
for what's the idol but a nothing?

1 CORINTHIANS 10:19, MSG

I have given up everything else—I have found it to be
the only way to really know Christ and to experience the
mighty power that brought him back to life again, and to
find out what it means to suffer and to die with him.

PHILIPPIANS 3:10, TLB

The link between love and obedience

Maybe you grew up with what felt like a lot of rules or a strict authority figure watching for you to step out of line. Some think it's the same way with God—that the Christian life is tiresome obedience to a long list of dos and don'ts. Yet Jesus said they can be summed up by just two: "Love the Lord your God with all your passion and prayer and intelligence" and "Love others as well as you love yourself" (Matthew 22:37, 39, MSG). In God's view, there is a link between love and obedience. God's rules are there because they're good for us—not to shame us. He doesn't want blind, rote obedience, but a willing giving of ourselves to his wisdom. Will you love him in this way?

All the other commandments . . . stem from these two laws and are fulfilled if you obey them. Keep only these and you will find that you are obeying all the others.

MATTHEW 22:40, TLB

This is love: that we walk in obedience to his commands. As you have heard from the beginning, his command is that you walk in love.

2 JOHN 1:6, NIV

No runnin' in the
house unless it's
on fire—and it better
be a hot one

Don't get above your raisin'

Remember where you came from

The bluegrass song with this title is about a man's girlfriend who seems to have gotten on her high horse and starts to look down on him. "Don't get above your raisin'," he warns her. Maybe God is singing this to you as well, reminding you not to forget how you started out. Often our early days as Christians are thrilling and exuberant because we know how much the Lord has rescued us from. But as time goes on, it's easy to become too full of ourselves, even kind of uppity. We forget how broken we once were and how we don't deserve the grace that God has given us. It might be time to sit humbly at God's feet and remember where you came from.

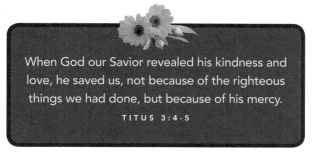

When God our Savior revealed his kindness and love, he saved us, not because of the righteous things we had done, but because of his mercy.

TITUS 3:4-5

Putting the devil in his place

The Bible talks a lot about taming our tongues and being moderate in our talk and careful in our actions. But there's one situation where God approves of giving down the country. Has the enemy been talking to you, spreading his lies and dangling temptations in front of you? He's a clever devil, he is. Well, there's no puttin' up with that. Give him a piece of your mind. Know that Jesus was tempted too. Echo his words: "Get away from me, Satan!" Give the devil a good talking-to, and push him out of your life.

Get away from me, Satan! You are a dangerous trap to me. You are seeing things merely from a human point of view, not from God's.

MATTHEW 16:23

The time for judging this world has come, when Satan, the ruler of this world, will be cast out. And when I am lifted up from the earth, I will draw everyone to myself.

JOHN 12:31-32

Only God can
give all of himself
to everyone

Stop trying to do it all

You're working so hard because you don't want to sit below the salt, and as a result, you're worn slap out. You need the money; you want to rise above; you desire the better life that more earnings might provide. But there's a limit to what's good for you. Know that God wants you to rest, to have a balanced life. He wants you to have some fun! Take time with him. Pray about your tendency to overwork. Listen to his whisper, and trust him to provide.

It is useless for you to work so hard from early morning until late at night, anxiously working for food to eat; for God gives rest to his loved ones.

PSALM 127:2

Don't wear yourself out trying to get rich. Be wise enough to know when to quit. In the blink of an eye wealth disappears, for it will sprout wings and fly away like an eagle.

PROVERBS 23:4-5

When you're stuck with no options

Do you feel like you've run into a brick wall? You've said to yourself, *Can't never could* and have given it your best. You've tried. But after pursuing this thing so hard and so long, you're stuck. It would make a lot of horse sense for you to pray about it. Not only to pray, but also to listen. Maybe God is telling you this is *not* the thing, *not* what you should go after. Or maybe, just maybe, he wants to show you what he can do to make you realize that with his help, you will overcome. After all, he is God. Know that with him, where there's a wall, there's a way.

Overwhelming victory is ours through Christ, who loved us.

ROMANS 8:37

You, dear children, are from God and have overcome . . . because the one who is in you is greater than the one who is in the world.

1 JOHN 4:4, NIV

His hogs are so
poor it takes six
of them to make
a shadow

Overcoming worries about money

Marty Stuart's hit song "Too Much Month (At the End of the Money)" paints a familiar picture. Bills, expenses, and costly repairs seem to strangle the life out of any financial cushion we hoped to enjoy. We simply don't know where the money will come from. It isn't about splurging on expensive things—often we worry about just getting by. Why doesn't God provide more? Well, maybe he wants us to come to him with our money worries. Perhaps he wants us to draw near and lean on him to provide. Jesus doesn't promise financial wealth or luxury, but he does promise everything one could ever need to those who seek him and do what's right. Will you trust him?

It is better to be godly and have little than to be evil and rich. For the strength of the wicked will be shattered, but the LORD takes care of the godly.

PSALM 37:16-17

Your storm will pass

Looking back on your childhood, do you remember waking up at night to the roaring rumble of a thunderstorm? Do you recall how scared you were? We're not so different today as adults. We go through the storms of life, and sometimes they're frightening. What kind of storm has interrupted your peace lately? Maybe you've been weathering a health crisis, a financial downturn, or the loss of a loved one. When thick clouds roll through and heavy winds threaten to knock you down, remember how Jesus walked on water amid raging winds. Recall that as he stepped into the boat with Peter, the wind calmed down. Know that Jesus won't abandon you either. Eventually your bad weather will pass. Brighter skies are yonder—it's fairin' off.

When you go through deep waters, I will be with you. When you go through rivers of difficulty, you will not drown.

ISAIAH 43:2

When [Jesus and Peter] got into the boat, the wind ceased. And those in the boat worshiped him, saying, "Truly you are the Son of God."

MATTHEW 14:32-33, NRSV

It's
fairin'
off

You are the light
of the world—but only
if your switch
is turned on

Rekindling faith's passion

Is it different now for you? As a new Christian, you were whole hog for Jesus. Your new life with Jesus was a bright floodlight for all to see. Now that light has dimmed. The electricity has been cut off. Well, it's important to remember not only that the Bible says we are the "light of the world" (Matthew 5:14) but also that the source of our light is Jesus. Maybe, just maybe, you've been away from your power source. Spend time with the Lord each day. Read his words to you. Talk with him in prayer. Watch how your light flickers back on as you walk with him again.

The Word [Jesus] gave life to everything that was created, and his life brought light to everyone. The light shines in the darkness, and the darkness can never extinguish it. . . . The one who is the true light, who gives light to everyone, was coming into the world.

JOHN 1:4-5, 9

Making a place for praise

The classic Southern menu for Thanksgiving Day might include ham instead of turkey, cornbread dressing, mac and cheese, and buttermilk biscuits. You might even find fried okra on the table. We enjoy the tradition, the football on TV, and all that food. But sometimes we forget the reason for it all—giving thanks. And here's something else to think about: Giving thanks isn't just for one day a year. When you think about who God is and all that he's done for us, it's really too wonderful to put into words. But you can still try! Make every day a thanksgiving to him.

Oh come, let us sing to the LORD! Let us shout joyfully to the Rock of our salvation. Let us come before His presence with thanksgiving; let us shout joyfully to Him with psalms. For the LORD is the great God, and the great King above all gods.

PSALM 95:1-3, NKJV

Always be joyful. Never stop praying. Be thankful in all circumstances, for this is God's will for you who belong to Christ Jesus.

1 THESSALONIANS 5:16-18

God's givin'
deserves our
thanksgivin'

Is the Lord wondering where you've been?

A story is told of a pastor who said to one of his church members, "You need to join the army of the Lord!" The man replied, "I'm already in the army of the Lord." The pastor frowned, then asked, "How come I don't see you except at Christmas and Easter?" The man whispered in reply, "I'm in the secret service." Does this sound like you? If the Lord is wondering where you've been, why not reintroduce yourself to him? Having a relationship with Jesus is an amazing thing, so treasure the opportunity to get to know him alongside your brothers and sisters at church. They also need you to share your unique gifts and talents with them. See you next week!

Let us not neglect our meeting together, as some people do, but encourage one another.

HEBREWS 10:25

God has given each of you a gift from his great variety of spiritual gifts. Use them well to serve one another.

1 PETER 4:10

Living beyond appearances

Cowboys talk about "throwing a wide loop with a short rope," referring to a person who's trying to impress but doesn't have the stuff to back up his claims. Is there someone like that in your life? Don't be swayed by those who strut big and put on swagger. Remember, God owns "the cattle on a thousand hills" (Psalm 50:10), and they don't. The Lord gets to wear the ten-gallon hat, so don't be intimidated by those who are all hat and no cattle. Aren't you glad that he's the One who's in charge?

Don't judge by his appearance or height, for I have rejected him. The LORD doesn't see things the way you see them. People judge by outward appearance, but the LORD looks at the heart.

1 SAMUEL 16:7

Yours, O LORD, is the greatness, the power, the glory, the victory, and the majesty. Everything in the heavens and on earth is yours, O LORD, and this is your kingdom. We adore you as the one who is over all things.

1 CHRONICLES 29:11

All hat
and no
cattle

The greatest
message ever
heard came from
an empty tomb

The miracle of God's amazing grace

The Gaithers' recording of "Amazing Grace" opens with a soulful harmonica that sounds like it came straight out of New Orleans. The lyrics for this classic hymn were penned almost 250 years ago, and the words are still revered throughout the world today. Yet many don't pay attention to how the words express the miracle of the gospel: that we are "wretches" lost in sin, blind to our own condition, and that Jesus suffered, died, and walked out of a tomb to save us from our despair. It's the greatest message you'll ever hear. If you've never received God's amazing grace, come and ask him for it now. Don't miss your chance to be made right with the Lord—to "have a whole and lasting life"!

This is how much God loved the world: He gave his Son, his one and only Son. And this is why: so that no one need be destroyed; by believing in him, anyone can have a whole and lasting life. God didn't go to all the trouble of sending his Son merely to point an accusing finger, telling the world how bad it was. He came to help, to put the world right again.

JOHN 3:16-17, MSG

Notes

SO POOR HE HAD A TUMBLEWEED AS A PET

"You might be a redneck if the Blue Book value of your truck goes up and down depending on how much gas it has in it." As quoted in Mark Shatz with Mel Helitzer, *Comedy Writing Secrets, 3rd Edition: The Best-Selling Guide to Writing Funny & Getting Paid for It* (Blue Ash, OH: Writer's Digest Books, 2016), https://www.google.com/books/edition/Comedy_Writing_Secrets/giFjDwAAQBAJ?hl=en&gbpv=1&dq=jeff+foxworthy+you+might+be+a+rdneck+if+the+blue+book+value+of+your+truck+goes+up+and+down+depending+on+how+much+gas+it+has+in+it&pg=PT157&printsec=frontcover.

DO YOUR BEST, AND GOD WILL DO THE REST

"Being a successful person is not necessarily defined by what you have achieved, but by what you have overcome." Fannie Flagg, *The All-Girl Filling Station's Last Reunion* (New York: Random House, 2014), 332.

A LOT OF KNEELIN' WILL KEEP YOU IN GOOD STANDIN'

"I convinced myself that normal rules did not apply. . . . I felt that I had worked hard my entire life and deserved to enjoy all the temptations around me." Steven Aicinena, "When Pride Goes Wrong," abstract, *Sport Journal* 21, August 19, 2011, https://thesportjournal.org/article/when-pride-goes-wrong/#post/0.

YOUR BESTEST FRIEND

See Jeanne Robertson, "Jeanne Robertson | Bestest Friend—Ring Guards," JeanneRobertson, December 2, 2015, YouTube video, 6:27, https://www.youtube.com/watch?v=OdKzdIWl51E.

WHAT IN TARNATION?!

See "The Dagnabbit Factor," The Word Detective, May 4, 2004, http://www.word-detective.com/050404.html.

A GRUDGE IS A HEAVY THING TO CARRY

"Someone once said, 'Resentment is like swallowing poison and waiting for the other person to die.'" The website Quote Investigator attributes the earliest iteration of this quote to Bert Ghezzi, *The Angry Christian* (Ann Arbor, MI: Servant, 1980), 99. See "Resentment Is like Taking Poison and Waiting for the Other Person to Die," Quote Investigator, August 19, 2017, https://quoteinvestigator.com/2017/08/19/resentment/.

GOD LOVE HER

"In the classic 1939 movie *Gone with the Wind*, Rhett Butler passionately tells Scarlett O'Hara, 'I love you more than I've ever loved any woman. And I've waited longer for you than I've ever waited for any woman.'" See "Gone with the Wind (4/6) Movie CLIP—Leaving for Battle (1939) HD," Movieclips, May 26, 2011, YouTube video, 2:42, https://www.youtube.com/watch?v=yNvuIuWY3Sw.

QUITTIN' COLD TURKEY

See "Why Do We Quit 'Cold Turkey'?" *Merriam-Webster*, accessed January 2, 2020, https://www.merriam-webster.com/words-at-play/why-do-we-quit-cold-turkey.

SHE'S AS HONEST AS THE DAY IS LONG

"You never know what's in a person's heart until they're tested, do you?" Mrs. Threadgoode in Fannie Flagg, *Fried Green Tomatoes at the Whistle Stop Cafe* (New York: Ballantine, 2016), 96.